Leigh, Tyldesley and A
A Bygone Era

Text by Peter Riley - Foreword by Tor

A collection of rare archive photographs of
Leigh, Tyldesley, Atherton, Golborne,
Abram, Glazebury, Astley and Hindley

P & D RILEY

First published 1994

**Published by P & D Riley,
12 Bridgeway East,
Windmill Hill,
Runcorn,
Cheshire WA7 6LD.**

Text (c) 1994 by Peter Riley
Foreword (c) 1994 by Tony Ashcroft
Photographs (c) by Wigan Metropolitan Borough Council

ISBN: 1 874712 13 1

ACKNOWLEDGEMENTS

The publishers and Wigan Heritage Service would like to thank all those who have given or loaned pictures to the archives, without whose generosity this look back into the past of the area would not be possible

Grateful thanks also to Len Hudson of the Archives Department of Wigan MBC for his patience, professionalism and generosity of time in producing copies of the photographs in this book. Also grateful thanks to Alastair Gillies of Wigan's Heritage Department for his co-operation and for permission to sift through the super photographic collection in the Archives Department, and to Tony Ashcroft, Local History Officer of Leigh Library for writing the foreword and for his enthusiasm for the project.

Thanks are also due to Alan Hulley of Chamleys Bookshop and to Dorothy Booker of LAMP Bookshop both in Leigh for their suppport and enthusiasm, and a special thanks to all those unknown photographers who had the foresight to take these wonderful pictures in the first place. Readers may also be interestd to know that copies of the photographs in the book as well as others in the archives collection can be ordered by writing to the Archives Department, Town Hall, Leigh.

Printed and bound in England by Manchester Free Press

FOREWORD

"Time passes. Listen. Time passes. Come closer now," says the first voice in Dylan Thomas's unique play for voices entitled 'Under Milk Wood'. Well, I am certain that most of us would agree with these sentiments. The times they are a changing very quickly indeed in this last decade of the twentieth century.

We appear to live in an instant society, where our wants can be satisfied almost immediately. Yet for all our cars, computers, television sets, videos, microwaves, cash dispensers and all the other indispensable items of our lives, who would, for a short time, not readily exchange our bustling and stressful existence for the more spacious days of our forebears?

Just for a moment then, let us slip back into the past with the help of this book of photographs chosen by Peter Riley from the large collecton held by Wigan Metropolitan Borough Council's Heritage Section. To a more younger generation the photographs may appear to be increasingly removed from today's experience of living, but nevertheless they can be a very valuable, rich and rewarding source for local history research and information, as well as being of interest in their own right.

It has been said that a photograph is worth a thousand words. There is also a power in it which has the ability to unlock our remembrances of times past, helps us to explain the present and to contemplate the future more positively.

Therefore open the book and enjoy these old photographs which I am positive will give you great pleasure as they bring the past to life.

TONY ASHCROFT
Local History Officer

Leigh

IN 1904 when this fine photograph was taken, any form of mechanised transport was still a novelty, and to the people standing at the corner of Bradshawgate, on the left, outside the old Rope and Anchor pub, the novelty was in the passing of the number 21 tram as it neared the junction with Railway Road. The bank building on the right is still there, but the church has long since disappeared, as have the buildings on the left of the picture.

Leigh

THIS photograph, of the junction of Bradshawgate, was taken in 1890 and shows the dilapidated but once popular Stirrups Fish Shop which stood on the corner for a good many years and which many locals frequented. Note, too, the massive poster advertising the Theatre Royal in Leigh which was a very popular music hall and which still exists today as a night club.

Leigh

MANY Leigh companies kept body and soul together by providing a very personal service to the town's residents, particularly those in need of such basics as shoes or clogs, and this fine picture, taken in the early 20s or 30s, shows a local clog shop on King Street. Of particular interest in this photograph is the building next door belonging to the Lilford Weaving Company. Besides showing the still busy traditional Lancashire industry, the company has a bracket for a telephone on the outside brickwork, and it must have been one of the earliest firms in Leigh to have a telephone.

Leigh

ALTHOUGH undated this photograph of three men and a trap in King Street, Leigh, shows fashions of around the 1920s and early 30s. Certainly the woman crossing the cobbled street shows a dress standard which we can see in early movies of the period. It is possible that this picture was taken on a Sunday or public holiday for the men seem particularly smartly dressed with the ubiquitous shiny shoes and are obviously waiting to set off on a day trip, and the man on the right seems to be holding a flask of some kind.

Leigh

WHAT a magical photograph of old Leigh this one is. Taken in 1897 it shows magnificent dray horses pulling a cart full of beer barrels from Chapel Street into Brewery Lane. The picture also shows the smaller but just as necessary presence of the 'rag and bone' man, for whom a visit could mean the difference between a clean front door step an a shabby one, for he was a popular supplier of the old donkey stones which housewives found so essential...and all for a few old rags!

Leigh

THIS photograph is a wonderful combination of Victorian and Edwardian Leigh, and shows a subtle but nevertheless changing scene on Bradshawgate. The horse drawn carriage or 'growler' in the forefront is of the Victorian age, as is the hansom cab in the distance, but the 20th century had arrived with the growing popularity of the bicycle as shown by the man on the left. Another bicycle is also just seen leaning against a wall on the right of the 'growler'. The fashions too show the changing decades with a combination of pavement length skirts, some just above ankle length and the very traditional shawls of old Lancashire as seen on the women to the left of the cyclist.

Leigh

IF this group of Leythers could only return to their town for a day what would they think of the traffic which now travels along this street a century after the picture was taken? This is Chapel Street, Leigh, pictured in 1890 and is a super example of a working class northern town, with its combination of carters, colliers, railway workers (the shiny buttons on the tall man walking towards the camera suggests this), and a rag tag of assorted workers. Note, though, the hat shop on the left, which attracted a women clientele of higher status than the average housewife in the town.

Leigh

TAKEN outside Joseph Isherwood's tripe dressing shop in King Street, Leigh, it would be interesting to know what was happening on this day in 1900. Was it a visit by travelling showmen, suggested by the minstrel faces on the left, or was it a horse show as suggested by the horseshoe display? One other possibility is a celebration of the new century. certainly the horses were well dressed for the event with their plumed manes, with many of the observers dressed in their best finery, including top hats and bowlers.

Leigh

THE year 1900 was just cause to celebrate the start of the 20th century, and with it the zenith of the British Empire, then the most powerful and richest in the world. But underneath the glamour and the wealth was a story of terrible deprivation, and this photograph showing King Street Workhouse in Leigh with one of its inmates does more to show the contrast than mere words.

Leigh

No. 33. POLICE COURTS. LEIGH.

MANY residents of Leigh in 1912 would have been familiar with this building, particularly if they had been unfortunate enough to appear before local magistrates. For this was the old Police Courts in Church Street, long since demolished and now used as a car park. The smaller building at the rear is still there though. This was originally the stables for police horses used by constables in the police station which then stood at the rear of the courts. This building is now used by the town's senior citizens as an information and recreation centre.

Leigh

THIS photograph was taken in Railway Road, Leigh, in 1947, outside Sems Cinema where an accident took place urgent enough to summon local town constables and attract the attention of local people, particularly children. How many of these children still live in Leigh and recall the incident? Incidentally, the poster on the wall shows the cinema was screening Bing Crosby and Bob Hope in the popular 'Road to Rio' movie. It's good bet the driver of this van wished he was on the road to South America too!

Leigh

MANY people in Leigh will remember this shop. This was T.C. Manfredi's ice cream shop, a magnet for many of the town's children. Although we don't have a date for this picture, the style of the dress suggests it could be the 1930s. The logo on the window read "Superior to Many, Equal to Any, Second to None". No doubt many of today's older generation who patronised the shop on Chapel Street, Leigh, would agree!

Leigh

IF anyone in Leigh cares to stand outside the Iceland Frozen Food store in Bradshawgate and look across the road they will see this building although they will probably not recognise it. This was the Lilford Hotel, a busy hotel catering for railway travellers to the town, and observant visitors can still see the faded outline of the hotel name on the building. The lower level has, of course, changed since it was converted to shop fronts. This good sized hotel shows the importance of Leigh as a centre of industry in the days when it was necessary for travellers to the town to stay overnight before the ascent of cars.

Leigh

BEECH Walk, Pennington, is still in the prosperous part of Leigh, about a mile or so from the town centre, but when this photograph was taken earlier this century the beech trees were still there. Alas, they have long gone, and the area no longer looks so rural as in this lovely scene.

Leigh

THIS photograph is not only interesting in its own right but is historically important too. For it is of the number 27 tram, the first tram to run through Leigh on King Street.

Leigh

THE Great War, better known as The First World War, was a terrible ordeal for Britain and no less for the 'volunteers' from Leigh who were called to arms to fight for King and Empire. Hundreds of thousands of British soldiers never returned, but this photograph taken in 1918 shows a group from Leigh at a special demobilisation session outside the Conservative Club in Railway Road.

Leigh

A FASCINATING photograph taken in Railway Road, Leigh, in 1907 showing a huge crowd gathering in front of the Leigh Journal newspaper office to celebrate the Golden Jubilee of the town's Co-operative movement. The verandah's may have been taken away but otherwise the facade of all these buildings remain the same today, much to the joy of local historians!

Leigh

ANOTHER photograph of the Leigh Journal office and the Bolton Evening News offices in Railway Road taken in 1967. Although taken 60 years after the previous picture the facade has not changed except for the removal of the verandah.

Leigh

THIS is an interesting photograph of Bradshawgate, Leigh, taken in the early 20th century before the road was widened to meet Railway Road. How peaceful the scene looks without a single vehicle in sight. The appearance of a photographer was still rare enough to attract a watching group of locals though!

Hindley

TAKEN in January 1940 this dramatic photograph of Market Street, Hindley shows that local people had more than mere warfare to cope with, they had one of the worst snowstorms of the period! The photograph shows the Palace Theatre which was advertising as its main attraction Lawrence Olivier in Wuthering Heights.

Hindley

TAKEN many years before the 1940 snowscene, this is Market Street, Hindley, around 1910 and is intriguing for showing what a huge attraction a street photographer was to local people.

Hindley

WHAT a mixture was Allens grocery shop in Moss Lane, Platt Bridge. For besides selling chocolate and general groceries the shop also boasted selling fried and chips, potatoes and of being a restaurant! Who were the two ladies posing for the picture?

Hindley

YET another scene of Market Street, Hindley taken in 1902 and what a telling scene it is. Besides the ubiquitous police constable on duty next to the wonderful lamp standard the picture also shows the town's steam tram and engine, one of the earliest of the era. And what a magnificent cobbled road!

Glazebury

WHAT a fabulous old photograph this is, taken around 1900 of a gang of road menders posing for the camera in Glazebury. This type of muscle racking labour was a far cry from the basically easy time had by workers today with the benefit of mechanised ditch diggers. It is possible these men lived locally and were employed by the local parish and their ancestors may still live in the village today.

Glazebury

THIS photograph was taken in 1929 at Glazebury Church of England All Saints Church, and is an interesting study in the social status of the village by comparing the standards of dress, particularly among the boys! It would be interesting to know if any of the boys and girls shown still live out their adult lives in the Glazebury area.

Glazebury

THIS is a fine example of a real community group of people, for this is Glazebury Brass Band pictured at the back of Leigh Town Hall sometime between 1910 and 1920.

Glazebury

FOR a study in a rural setting which would have suited Thomas Hardy this photograph of Warrington Road, Glazebury, would take some beating. It is difficult to imagine the serenity of the scene today with the stream of constant traffic which passes this spot. The white building in the distance is the popular George and Dragon public house which hasn't altered much from the outside. The cottage on the right was obviously used by the village wheelwright.

Glazebury

MANY Glazebury residents will know this building. For this is the Foresters Arms, a pub popular when this shot was taken in the early years of the 20th century, and still popular today although much altered to suit modern trends of pub visitors.

Glazebury

THE George and Dragon pub in Glazebury has always been a popular drinking spot for locals and visitors alike, but when this photograph was taken it was locals who made up the majority of drinkers and they were invited to get into the photograph with landlord William Harvey (probably the man on the far left without a jacket) and his staff. The men are all wearing hats with the exception of Mr. Harvey and another man who is probably his barman. Maybe some locals can still identify the people as their long gone relatives.

Glazebury

PUBLIC houses feature heavily in the small community of Glazebury even today, and times have not changed much. They have been a focus of community spirit for centuries and in this picture of the Chat Moss Hotel taken, it is thought, in 1911 to celebrate the coronation of George V the patriotic spirit is obvious.

Tyldesley

THOUGH not a busy scene this photograph of the old Tyldesley Railway Station taken in 1926 is still of historical interest, for it shows not only the type of motor car then commonly in use, but also shows the station and line were then owned by the London and North Western Railway Company.

Tyldesley

FROM train and cars to buses, and this fine shot taken in Tyldesley in 1955 shows the attention caused when this Lancashire United Transport bus to Nook Pits ended up in Pit Lodge.

Tyldesley

THIS photograph of Elliott Street, Tyldesley, taken early in the 20th century must rate as one of the most interesting pictures of the town at that time. It clearly shows the unique shoe sign of the local cobbler above the shop owned by Bainbridge the local fruit dealer as well as showing Tyldesley Town Hall. And what a fascinating social scene too!

Tyldesley

ELEVEN ladies and one male driver must have made for a unique excursion when this picture was taken in the 1920s. This formidable bunch were well wrapped with hats, scarves and top coats ready for a ladies day out from the Colliers Arms in Tyldesley.

Tyldesley

ALTHOUGH undated this photograph of Elliott Street, Tyldesley, was probably taken in the late 1950s or early 1960s judging by the type of cars then on the roads and the style of dress. The street on the right is Wareing Street, and drivers must wish that roads were still as quiet as this.

Tyldesley

THE photographer who took this magical picture must have had a foresight of knowing he was recording living history, for what a tremendous photograph of a group of Tyldesley Urban District Council road sweepers this is. Taken at the corner of Shuttle Street and Milk Street the picture is undated but is probably in the 1940s. The men were all wearing clogs and possibly lived locally.

Tyldesley

TRADITIONAL images of blacksmiths were of brawny, muscular men, but the image was not necessarily true, and this photograph shows Tyldesley's last blacksmith, George Pearson, hard at work and it is a photograph that local historians will long treasure.

Tyldesley

ALTHOUGH this old photograph of a parade in Tyldesley is undated, research suggests it was taken before 1901 and it is likely to be in celebration of some phase of the Boer War. Certainly there was a patriotic fervour in the air if the Union flags are anything to go by. The crowd were certainly dressed in their best finery, and the uniform of members of Tyldesley Fire Brigade on the first float was sparkling.

Tyldesley

PATRIOTISM was always a part of British life despite pretensions to the contrary, and this fine photograph of Ward Brothers clothiers taken in July 1913 at their shop on the corner of Stanley Street and Elliott Street, Tyldesley, proves the point. The shop front is adorned with flags and photographs of King George V and Queen Mary were were making a royal visit to the area.

Tyldesley

WITH a world war raging and the onslaught of German air attacks to cope with the demand on human resources was great in small places such as Tyldesley, and this photograph, taken in Upper George Street in 1942, shows the town's Air Raid Wardens ready for action.

Tyldesley

AS the Second World War dragged on it became important to collect as much cash as possible for the war effort and this photograph was taken in Tyldesley's Market Square in 1943 during War Savings Week.

Tyldesley

WHAT a wonderful atmospheric photograph of Tyldesley this is! Taken at the turn of the century it again shows a patriotic spirit in the town, but far more important historically is the wonderful sense of 'period' the costumes of men, women and children show with the majesty of law marching confidently down the middle of the road in the shape of two huge Bobbies.

Tyldesley

ANOTHER undated photograph but certainly early in the 20th century and showing a walking day in Tyldesley

Astley

PIT work was always hard and workers did not always enjoy the benefits of better conditions experienced in the Lancashire coalfields in later years, and this photograph shows the hardship in the faces of workers at Mosley Common Pit. The fascinating thing about this picture is the smallness of so many of the pit workers and the obvious tender ages of many of them.

Astley

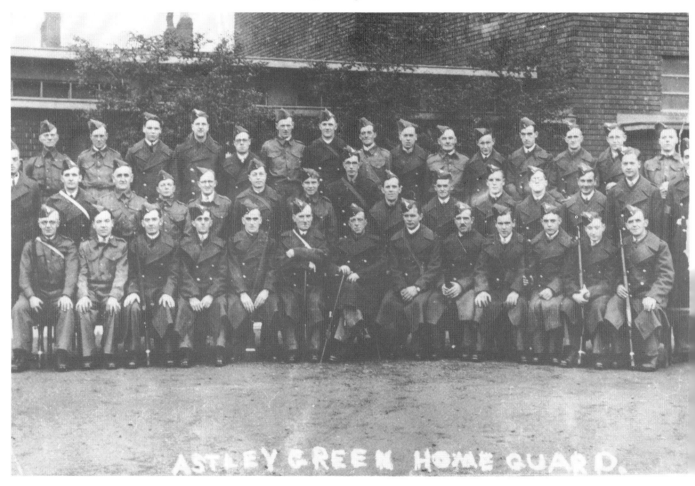

WHEN the Second World War continued to rage it became necessary to form some type of local defence force, normally from those either not able-bodied enough to serve in the regular forces or who were left at home because of their age or the importance of their job, and this photograph shows Astley Green Home Guard Unit in full uniform, which probably dates it in the 1942-43 period.

Astley

THE number 53 bus between Astley and Tyldesley was the first to run between the two areas, and this peculiar shaped bus is pictured getting ready for its first trip in 1920 at The Straits, watched by local police constables.

Astley

THIS photograph was taken in July 1919 outside Astley Methodist Chapel and shows a group of local nurses joining in Astley's peace celebrations following the ending of the First World War.

Astley

ALTHOUGH hundreds of thousands of British men failed to return from the battlefields of France after the Great War, those who did return were happy to celebrate their victory over the Hun. This picture shows local people turning out in force to take part in Astley Peace Day in Higher Green in August 1919.

Astley

THIS is a wonderful photograph with plenty of atmosphere of a once busy occupation which would have done Henry Hobson of Hobson's Choice proud! It is a scene inside Mr Fearnley's Clog Shop in Astley taken in 1910.

Golborne

LEGH ST. GOLBORNE.

ALTHOUGH no date accompanies this photograph it is almost certainly around the 1900-1910 era if the dress of the young ladies is anything to go by. The man near the lamp post also has the look of a Charlie Chaplin about him, but this wasn't early century Hollywood, it was Legh Street, Golborne.

Golborne

SIMILAR yet different is one way to describe this scene of High Street, Golborne, taken at the turn of the century. Although things change, such as the disappearance of the cobbled road and the gas lamps, the scene still retains to this day a feeling of familiarity and a village like atmosphere.

Golborne

LOCAL shops in Golborne have always prided themselves on supplying a comprehensive service to their customers and this shop belonging to J. Beswick and Son in High Street was no exception. Supplying, as it did, hardware and fishing tackle, the range offered was astonishing and it is a pity the men in the picture are not identified.

Golborne

ANOTHER shop which provided almost everything anyone needed in the fruit and vegetables line was Barrows shop in High Street, Golborne, pictured here in 1908. The advertisement on the wall is interesting, advertising the White Star Line, boasting it owned the largest steamers in the world. A strange place for a shipping company to ply its trade!

Golborne

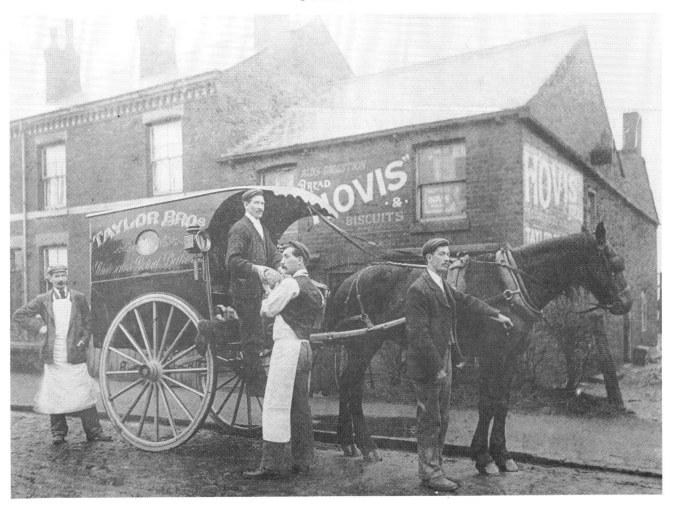

THIS photograph was taken outside the premises of Taylor Brothers at 32 Lowton Road, Golborne in 1890 and is a fascinating social scene of the era. Besides offering their own freshly baked bread, the company obviously were firm believers in the benefit of 'Hovis', which is still popular today. The boast then however, was that 'Hovis' was an aid to digestion.

Abram

IN August 1908 Abram suffered one of its worst disasters when 76 miners lost their lives at the Maypole Pit, and this picture dramatically shows the trauma of a rescue party returning from below no. 2 pit. It is probably correct to speculate that these men are the ancestors of people still living in the area today.

Abram

MAYPOLE COLLIERY DISASTER WAITING FOR NEWS.
AUG 18th 1908. No 2.

In any small community a pit disaster was always a personal tragedy for the whole community and in Abram the Maypole disaster was no exception. This tremendous photograph taken on August 18, 1908 shows local people outside the pit waiting for news.

Abram

ONLY 29 pictures were displayed on this poster depicting the colliery explosion at the Maypole pit in Abram in 1908, but the disaster killed 76 miners with only 3 being rescued alive. Even today, almost 90 years later, the disaster is still a talking point among the local people.

WITHOUT the glamour of today's media, such as television and full colour newspaper advertising, companies earlier this century had to rely on visual displays in their shop premises and the Abram branch of the Co-operative Wholesale Society was no exception, as shown in this unusual photograph.

Atherton

PROBABLY dating from the 1920s or early 30s this fine scene shows Market Street, Atherton. Note the traditional Lancashire shawl around the shoulders of some of the older women.

Atherton

THIS is a fine period photograph of Atherton although in historical terms it is not that old. Taken in Market Street in either the late 50s or early 60s it is interesting for showing the transition period between the popular trolley bus on the right and the up and coming motor bus which superceded it.

Atherton

DESPITE the Great Depression which swept the world in the 1930s there was still an attempt at keeping pupils fit in schools, and this photograph shows the 1935-36 gym team from Hesketh Fletcher School in Atherton.

Atherton

Market Street, Atherton.

ANOTHER photograph of Market Street, Atherton, taken, it is thought, in the 1930s. Again the Lancashire shawl is in evidence and it is worth noting just how quiet this now extremely busy road then was, with just a tram line to show it was used by vehicles at all.

Atherton

TRANSPORT has always been important to local people and Atherton is no exception. But transport in the early years of the 20th century was limited to horses and bicycles. That meant necessary and important work for the local blacksmith and this period photograph was taken in 1920 at the forge of S. Yates of Market Street, Atherton, which stood opposite the parish church.

Atherton

A STRANGE photograph probably taken sometime in the 1930s looking across at the obelisk in Atherton looking down Tyldesley Road from Market Street. The appearance of a barrel-organ in the distance did not seem to have attracted any attention even from those lounging around the monument.

Atherton

YET another fabulous photograph which unfortunately is undated, but showing a super team of horses and a stagecoach outside the Albion Inn in Atherton where the landlord was then James Banks. Obviously laid on for some very special occasion, the passengers seem a mixed bunch who were out to enjoy themselves.

Atherton

A PANORAMIC shot taken on August 9, 1947, of Atherton and clearly showing the town's traditional Lancashire image of back yards with outside lavatories, some yars with washing on the clothes line, and in the distance the parish church and some of the town's mills.

Atherton

ANOTHER fascinating photograph taken early in the 20th century showing delivery boys employed by James Shaw the baker and grocer of 40 Market Street, Atherton, Having to manhandle this cart through the cobbled streets to make deliveries was a far cry from the delivery bikes used by grocers' boys a generation later.

Atherton

POOR conditions were common enough in many local schools until very recent years, but that did not stop good teaching methods and a sturdy spirit among pupils, and despite the ominous presence of a large crack in the wall behind them, these children from Laburnum Street Infants School in Atherton appear unperturbed and attentive, and how neat and tidy they look too!

Atherton

TAKEN in a classroom at Chowbent School, Atherton, in 1895 this is a rare photograph showing a Victorian class posing for the camera. Although the appearance of the photographer was probably a welcome diversion from their lesson on the circulation of the blood, the imposing presence of their headteacher Isaich Barker at the back was obviously enough to keep these children dutifully stern.